BRENT LIBRARIES

Please return/renew this item
by the last date shown.
Books may also be renewed by
phone or online.
Tel: 0333 370 4700
On-line www.brent.gov.uk/libraryservice

FIRST
SPORTS
FACTS

VOLLEYBALL

RULES, EQUIPMENT AND KEY PLAYING TIPS

by Tyler Omoth

raintree
a Capstone company — publishers for children

Raintree is an imprint of Capstone Global Library Limited, a company incorporated in England and Wales having its registered office at 264 Banbury Road, Oxford, OX2 7DY – Registered company number: 6695582

www.raintree.co.uk
myorders@raintree.co.uk

Edited by Bradley Cole
Designed by Sarah Bennett and Katy LaVigne, media res
Picture research by Eric Gohl
Production by Kathy McColley
Originated by Capstone Global Library Limited
Printed and bound in China

ISBN 978-1-4747-5015-8
21 20 19 18 17
10 9 8 7 6 5 4 3 2 1

British Library Cataloguing in Publication Data
A full catalogue record for this book is available from the

Acknowledgements
We would like to thank the following for permission to re
Herald, 11; iStockphoto: FatCamera, 21 (left); Newscom: (
Lewis, 17, ZUMA Press/Allen Eyestone, 20 (left), ZUMA Press/Jon-Michael Sullivan, 21 (right), ZUMA Press/St Petersburg Times, 7; Shutterstock: A_Lesik, 1 (background, middle), Aspen Photo, 5, Daimond Shutter, cover (background), 1 (background, top left), Dean Harty, 1 (background, top right), Jan Kranendonk, 9 (bottom), MediaPictures.pl, 19, Mitrofanov Alexander, 1, muzsy, 20 (right), Paolo Bona, cover, 9 (top), Valeria Cantone, 15

Design Elements
Shutterstock

We would like to thank Tyler Omoth for his invaluable help in the preparation of this book.

CONTENTS

Time to attack!

Professional volleyball players work together to set up the perfect shot. Get ready to jump and **attack** the ball like Olympic volleyball star Kim Hill. If you enjoy action and teamwork, volleyball could be the sport for you.

ORIGINS OF VOLLEYBALL

In 1895 William G. Morgan wanted a sport for young businessmen in Massachusetts, USA. He wanted something that would not have as much physical contact as basketball. He used a tennis net and raised it just above the players' heads.

FACT

The International Volleyball Hall of Fame is located in Massachusetts, USA, where the game was invented.

attack jump and hit the volleyball over the net in a downward motion

CHAPTER 1

Ready to play!

Equipment

Volleyball is a sport that doesn't need a lot of equipment. The net, a ball and proper shoes are the most basic pieces. Volleyball players jump a lot during a play, so they need good shoes with lots of padding. They also dive to the ground to hit the ball. Some players wear knee pads for protection.

FACT

A volleyball player may jump as many as 100 times during a match.

"Coaches and players should keep a sense of humour. The bottom line is for the coach and the team to have fun and enjoy the sport."

– *Walt Ker, volleyball coach*

The volleyball court

A standard volleyball court is a large rectangle. Across the middle is the volleyball net. The top of the net is 2.2 metres (7.33 feet) high for women's competitions and 2.4 metres (7.97 ft) high for men's. Each side of the court has an **attack line**. The outside edges of the court are marked by **boundary lines**. Behind the back boundary line is the **service area**.

FACT
Volleyball became an Olympic team sport in 1964. The Soviet Union won the first men's gold medal. Japan won the first women's gold medal.

attack line line that divides the back row players from the front row players
boundary line line that marks the outside edge of the court
service area place where the server stands when putting the ball into play

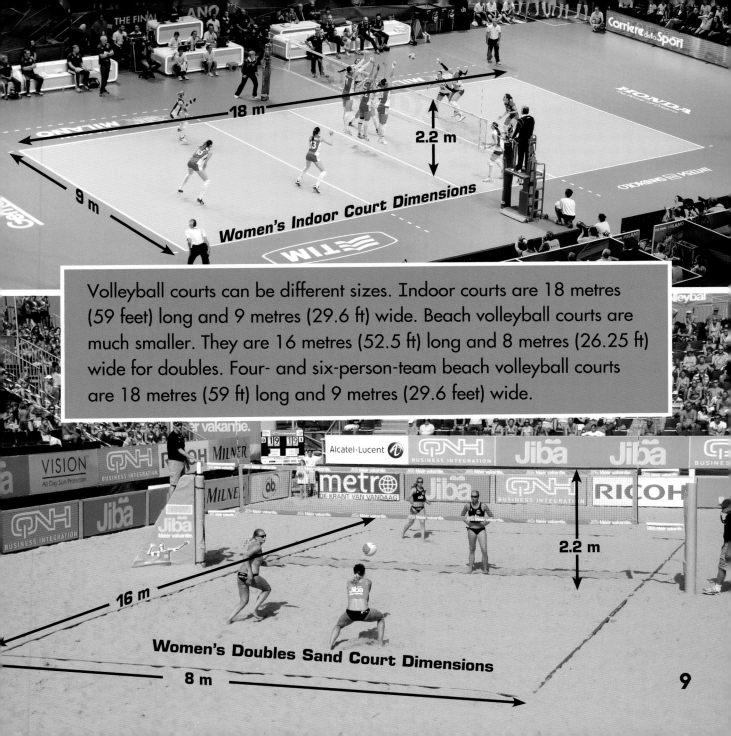

18 m

2.2 m

9 m

Women's Indoor Court Dimensions

Volleyball courts can be different sizes. Indoor courts are 18 metres (59 feet) long and 9 metres (29.6 ft) wide. Beach volleyball courts are much smaller. They are 16 metres (52.5 ft) long and 8 metres (26.25 ft) wide for doubles. Four- and six-person-team beach volleyball courts are 18 metres (59 ft) long and 9 metres (29.6 feet) wide.

2.2 m

16 m

Women's Doubles Sand Court Dimensions

8 m

The positions

A volleyball team has six players on the court at a time. Hitters are best at attacking the ball and hitting it over the net. Setters pass the ball to the hitters. Middle blockers work to **block** the other team's shots. They also need to be good attackers. A libero player may enter and leave the back row as often as needed.

FACT
The United States, Brazil and the former Soviet Union are tied for the most Olympic Gold medals in men's indoor volleyball with three medals each.

block attempt by a front row player to stop a spiked ball as it crosses the net

Middle Blocker

Libero

Hitter

Setter

CHAPTER 2

How the game works

Serving

Serving is a very important part of volleyball. The serve starts play. The server may choose an **overhand serve** or an **underhand serve**. Underhand serves are easier to do. They are also easier for the defence to receive. Overhand serves are difficult, but a good one could get your team an **ace**. If the ball touches the ground on the other side, your team scores a point!

overhand serve serving the ball by striking it above the head using a fast, throwing motion

underhand serve serving the ball by striking it with an underhand swing, using the heel of the hand

ace serve that hits the ground on the other team's side, giving your team a point

Types of hits

There are several ways to hit a volleyball. A **forearm pass** uses both arms. The player has clasped hands and holds them near the waist. The ball bounces off the player's arms below the elbows. A **set** is used when the ball is coming down above a player's head. A player uses their fingers to push the ball to a teammate. When the other team tries to hit the ball back over the net, a player may block it at the net.

forearm pass pass made by using the forearms

14 **set** pass directed to another teammate who will attack the ball

Attacking

The team with the ball is attacking. They try to hit the ball so that the other team can't return it over the net. Setters pass the ball high so a hitter can attack it. The hitter tries to hit the ball to part of the court where the other team's players can't reach it.

The team that wins 3 out of 5 sets of a volleyball match wins. The first four sets play to 25 points. If a match goes to the fifth set, it only plays to 15.

Defending

The defence tries to keep the ball off the ground on their side. Each team can only hit the ball three times each time it comes to their side. A block does not count as a hit. Players in the front row try to block the ball. Players in the back row try to pass the ball with a forearm pass.

FACT
In the 1920s volleyball became popular on the beach. Olympic beach volleyball teams have two players and slightly different rules. It became an official Olympic sport in 1996.

Now that you know the basics, it's time to start practising. Here are some tips to get you started.

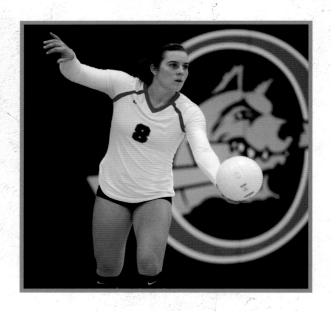

SERVING

Create a routine when serving. Bounce the ball, take a deep breath, toss the ball and strike! A set routine can make it easier to be consistent.

PASSING

Clasp your hands together, and turn your forearms up. You want to make a nice, flat surface for the ball to hit. Don't hit the ball with your hands. Let it hit your forearms.

SETTING

Try to get under the ball before it comes down. That way, you can hit the ball back up and to where you want it to go.

ATTACKING

The key to attacking the ball is timing. Practise jumping as a teammate sets the ball to you. You want to hit it just as you get above the net.

FACT

Bulgarian volleyball player Matey Kaziyski could hit a ball really hard. A ball he served was recorded going 132 kilometres (82 miles) per hour.

Glossary

ace   serve that hits the ground on the other team's side, giving your team a point

attack   jump and hit the volleyball over the net in a downward motion

attack line   line that divides the back row players from the front row players

block   attempt by a front row player to stop a spiked ball as it crosses the net

boundary line   line that marks the outside edge of the court

forearm pass   pass made by using the forearms

match   set of up to five volleyball games; to win a match, a team must win three games

overhand serve   serving the ball by striking it above the head using a fast, throwing motion

service area   place where the server stands when putting the ball into play

set   pass directed to another teammate who will attack the ball

underhand serve   serving the ball by striking it with an underhand swing, using the heel of the hand

Read more

Children's Book of Sport, DK (DK Children, 2011)

Look Inside Sports (Usborne Look Inside), Rob Lloyd Jones (Usborne Publishing Ltd, 2013)

The Science Behind Football, Volleyball, Cycling and Other Popular Sports (Science of the Summer Olympics), Stephanie Watson (Raintree, 2016)

Websites

www.bbc.com/sport/volleyball
Get the latest news about the sport.

www.volleyballengland.org/
Learn more about the official volleyball governing body of England.

www.volleyballengland.org/getintovolleyball/clubs
Find a volleyball club near you!

Index